New Careers for the
21st Century:
Finding Your Role in
the Global Renewal

MEDICAL TECHNICIANS:

HEALTH-CARE SUPPORT FOR THE

21ST CENTURY

New Careers for the 21st Century: Finding Your Role in the Global Renewal

New Careers for the
21st Century:
Finding Your Role in
the Global Renewal

MEDICAL TECHNICIANS:

HEALTH-CARE SUPPORT FOR THE

21ST CENTURY

by Cordelia Strange

Mason Crest Publishers

MEDICAL TECHNICIANS:

HEALTH-CARE SUPPORT FOR THE 21ST CENTURY

MASON CREST PUBLISHERS INC.
370 Reed Road
Broomall, Pennsylvania 19008
(866)MCP-BOOK (toll free)
www.masoncrest.com

9 8 7 6 5 4 3 2

Library of Congress Cataloging-in-Publication Data

Strange, Cordelia.
  Medical technicians : health-care support for the 21st century / by Cordelia Strange.
        p. cm. — (New careers for the 21st century : finding your role in America's renewal)
  Includes bibliographical references and index.
  ISBN 978-1-4222-1817-4   ISBN 978-1-4222-1811-2 (series)
  ISBN 978-1-4222-2038-2 (ppb)   ISBN 978-1-4222-2032-0 (series ppb)
  1. Biomedical technicians—Vocational guidance—Juvenile literature. I. Title.
  R856.25.S77 2011
  610.28023—dc22
                                          2010014934

Produced by Harding House Publishing Service, Inc.
www.hardinghousepages.com
Interior design by MK Bassett-Harvey.
Cover design by Torque Advertising + Design.
Printed in USA by Bang Printing.

CONTENTS

INTRODUCTION

Be careful as you begin to plan your career.

To get yourself in the best position to begin the career of your dreams, you need to know what the "green world" will look like and what jobs will be created and what jobs will become obsolete. Just think, according to the Bureau of Labor Statistics, the following jobs are expected to severely decline by 2012:

- word processors and data-entry keyers

- stock clerks and order fillers

- secretaries

- electrical and electronic equipment assemblers

- computer operators

- telephone operators

- postal service mail sorters and processing-machine operators

- travel agents

These are just a few of the positions that will decrease or become obsolete as we move forward into the century.

You need to know what the future jobs will be. How do you find them? One way is to look where money is being invested. Many firms and corporations are now making investments in startup and research enterprises. These companies may become the "Microsoft" and "Apple" of the twenty-first century. Look at what is being researched and what technology is needed to obtain the results.

Green world, green economy, green technology—they all say the same things: the way we do business today is changing. Every industry will be shaped by the world's new focus on creating a sustainable lifestyle, one that won't deplete our natural and economic resources.

The possibilities are unlimited. Almost any area that will conserve energy and reduce the dependency on fossil fuels is open to new and exciting career paths. Many of these positions have not even been identified yet and will only come to light as the technology progresses and new discoveries are made in the way we use that technology. And the best part about this is that our government is behind us. The U.S. government wants to help you get the education and training you'll need to succeed and grow in this new and changing economy. The U.S. Department of Labor has launched a series of initiatives to support and promote green job creation. To view the report, visit: www.dol.gov/dol/green/ earthday_reportA.pdf.

The time to decide on your future is now. This series, NEW CAREERS FOR THE 21ST CENTURY: FINDING YOUR ROLE IN THE GLOBAL RENEWAL, can act as the first step toward your continued education, training, and career path decisions. Take the first steps that will lead you—and the planet—to a productive and sustainable future.

Mike Puglisi
Department of Labor, District I Director (New York/New Jersey)
IAWP (International Association of Workforce Professionals)

It is the first of all problems for a [person] to find out what kind of work he [or she] is to do in this universe.

—Thomas Carlyle

CHAPTER 1
WHAT DO MEDICAL TECHNICIANS DO?

Words to Know

Epidemiologist: A scientist who studies the sources, appearance of, and amount of disease in large populations.

Bachelor's degree: The degree given to a student who completes four years of undergraduate studies; also known as a baccalaureate degree.

Master's degree: The degree awarded to a student who has completed at least one year of graduate study.

Automation: The process of controlling a process or operating a device with machines and minimum human intervention.

Analytical: Pertaining to the investigation and study of a problem.

Cultures: Growths of microorganisms, like bacteria, used to discover the source of an infection or used in labs for study.

Pathologists: The scientists who study and diagnose diseases by examining their causes and development in bodies (organs, tissues, and bodily fluids).

Infectious: Capable of being passed from one person to another, as a disease.

What comes to mind when you think of medicine? Do you picture a doctor reading charts and diagnosing mysterious diseases, or a nurse leaning over a bedside, cooling a fevered brow? While doctors and nurses dominate most popular images of the medical industry, they are not the only two options for a student interested in a health care career. Dentist, pharmacist, veterinarian, *epidemiologist*, and bioengineer are just some of the many other career options available in the health care industry.

Many of these career options involve working closely with patients, but there are also many behind-the-scenes workers. Medical laboratory technicians work in laboratories, running tests and helping doctors diagnose diseases. These laboratory technicians often use specialized instruments, laboratory equipment, and computers. Emergency medical technicians are trained to respond and perform basic lifesaving procedures during medical emergencies. Medical records technicians specialize in medical record keeping and health care information access.

Did You Know?
The Bureau of Labor Statistics estimates that from 2006–2016 there will be a need for 4,883,000 new workers in the healthcare industry.

Which medical technician career is right for you?

CHOOSING THE RIGHT CAREER

The young adults of today will be the job force of tomorrow, so choosing a career that will best fit with the needs of the changing world will be important to both job satisfaction and a successful life. With the vast array of career and job options, it is important for young adults to understand which work will be the best match for their interests, talents, goals, and personality types. If you are interested in medicine and enjoy laboratory work, a career as a medical technician might be right for you.

Certain job industries are expected to gain importance within the early decades of the twenty-first century. According to the United States Bureau of Labor Statistics, the number of jobs across all industries is expected to increase by 11 percent through the year 2018, while the number of jobs for medical technology is expected to increase by as much as 26 percent. In fact, in a list of the top-fifty in-demand healthcare jobs, different specializations of medical technicians appear numerous times.

Occupation Title (Sorted Initially by Projected Need) *Sort by*	Projected Need for Employees (2006 - 2016) *Sort by*	Projected Growth *Sort by*	2008 Hourly Wage Range[2] *Sort by (Median)*			Education & Training[3] *Sort by (College degree)*		
			Bottom 10%	Median	Top 10%	High School or less	Some College	College degree or higher
Personal and Home Care Aides — Description, State Report	519,000	27+%	$7	$9	$12	58%	31%	11%
Home Health Aides — Description, State Report	454,000	27+%	$8	$10	$14	57%	35%	8%
Medical Assistants — Description, State Report	199,000	27+%	$10	$14	$19	34%	54%	12%
Substance Abuse and Behavioral Disorder Counselors — Description, State Report	45,000	27+%	$12	$18	$29	9%	16%	75%
Pharmacy Technicians — Description, State Report	178,000	27+%	$9	$13	$19	30%	53%	17%
Physical Therapist Assistants — Description, State Report	27,000	27+%	$14	$22	$31	14%	66%	20%
Dental Hygienists — Description, State Report	82,000	27+%	$21	$32	$44	3%	62%	35%
Mental Health and Substance Abuse Social Workers — Description, State Report	62,000	27+%	$10	$18	$30	8%	16%	76%
Mental Health Counselors — Description, State Report	50,000	27+%	$11	$18	$30	9%	16%	75%
Marriage and Family Therapists — Description, State Report	12,000	27+%	$13	$21	$34	9%	16%	75%

Health careers in general are expected to have excellent job opportunities over the next decade. This chart lists the top ten in-demand health care jobs, sorted by projected growth. Medical technology just misses this list with a slightly lower projected growth of 26 percent.

MEDICAL TECHNICIANS

A student interested in training to be a medical technician has a number of career paths from which to choose. Each career path involves different education and training requirements. Some technicians are qualified to begin work with a two-year degree from a community college. Other positions require a *bachelor's degree* or even a *master's degree*. Understanding what each of the types of technicians does will help guide a student to the best education track.

CLINICAL LABORATORY TECHNOLOGISTS AND TECHNICIANS

Clinical laboratory technicians, also know as medical technicians and clinical laboratory technologists, or clinical laboratory scientists, play an important role in the detection, diagnosis, and treatment of disease.

Clinical laboratory workers examine and analyze body fluids and cells. They perform tests looking for bacteria, parasites, and other microorganisms; analyze the chemical content of fluids; match blood for transfusions; and test for drug levels in the blood that show how a patient is responding to treatment.

Technologists prepare samples for examination, count cells, and look for abnormal cells (such as cancer cells) in blood and body fluids. They use many different types of laboratory equipment, such as microscopes, and cell counters. They also use instruments that can complete a number of tests at the same time. After testing and examining a specimen, technologists analyze the results and send them to physicians.

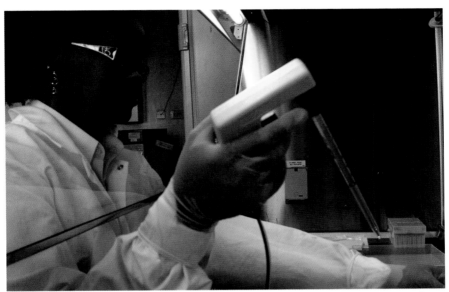

Working with blood, other bodily fluids, and diseases can raise some safety concerns. This laboratory technician is working behind a hood to protect herself from harm as well as to keep the sample as free from contamination as possible.

Because of *automation* and the use of computer technology, the work of technologists and technicians has become less hands-on and more *analytical*. The complexity of tests performed, the level of judgment needed, and the amount of responsibility depend largely on the amount of education and experience a technician or technologist has. Usually, technologists are given more responsibility than technicians; some technologists supervise technicians.

CLINICAL LABORATORY TECHNOLOGISTS

Clinical laboratory technologists perform complex tests, examine blood and other body fluids, and make *cultures* to determine the presence of bacteria, fungi, parasites, or other microorganisms. Technologists analyze samples for chemical content or a chemical reaction and determine concentrations of compounds such as blood glucose and cholesterol levels. They also ensure the accuracy of tests by evaluating test results, modifying procedures, and monitoring programs.

In smaller labs, technologists perform a wide range of tests, but in larger labs they are likely to specialize in a certain type of procedure. These specialized technologists are named for the task they perform:

- Clinical chemistry technologists prepare specimens and analyze the chemical and hormonal contents of body fluids.

- Microbiology technologists examine and identify bacteria and other microorganisms.

- Blood bank technologists, or immunohematology technologists, collect, type, and prepare blood and its components for transfusions.

- Immunology technologists examine elements of the human immune system and its response to foreign bodies.

- Cytotechnologists prepare slides of body cells and examine these cells microscopically for abnormalities that may signal the beginning of a cancerous growth.

- Molecular biology technologists perform complex protein and nucleic acid testing on cell samples.

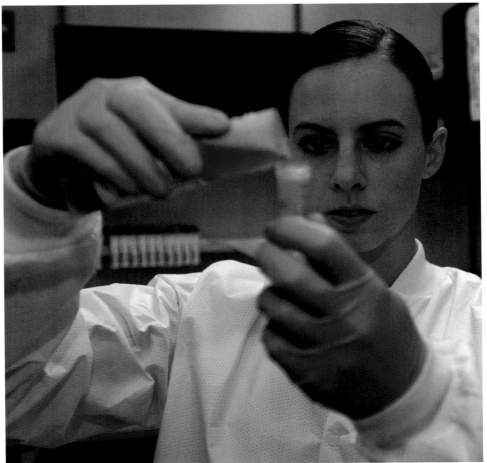

Medial technicians generally perform simple lab work under the supervision of the more highly trained technologists. This technician may be preparing a sample for analysis by a technologist or perhaps for automated analysis.

CLINICAL LABORATORY TECHNICIANS

Clinical laboratory technicians perform simpler tests and laboratory procedures than technologists. Technicians prepare specimens, operate automated analyzers, or perform manual tests,

Phlebotomists are special technicians who collect blood samples from patients. Each specimen is carefully labeled and coded to indicate the patient and what test is supposed to be run on that sample.

usually under the supervision of technologists or laboratory managers. Like technologists, clinical laboratory technicians may work in several areas of the clinical laboratory or specialize in just one. For example:

• Phlebotomists collect blood samples.

• Histotechnicians cut and stain tissue specimens for microscopic examination by *pathologists*.

WORK ENVIRONMENT

Clinical laboratory technicians and technologists work with *infectious* specimens, but with proper safety precautions and clothing,

Real Life Medical Technician

Maritza Sinclair is lead medical records technician at the National Institutes of Health (NIH) in Bethesda, Maryland. She chose the career because it matched her interests and education. Her original education and training was through the Army Reserves as a licensed practical nurse (LPN), but she found the career more frustrating than satisfying.

Maritza sent out a bunch of applications for a more administrative position and was hired part-time by the NIH. After some basic on-the-job training about the patient record numbering system, she was hired full-time. Some of her regular tasks include:

- Pulling patient records—"In the morning, I ensure that the list of patient records (what we call the pull list) are pulled and ready for delivery to the appropriate clinic."
- Staff reassignments—"If one of our staff is out, I rearrange the schedule and make reassignments to cover that person's duties."
- Collecting additional records—"Many patients at the NIH are referred from other clinical centers or hospitals. . . . I am responsible for making sure that the records from outside sources get into their NIH patient record."
- Retrieving records—"Often in the afternoon, I go to clinics to retrieve files that were pulled earlier in the day."
- Calculating monthly statistics—"I prepare monthly statistics of all the records released to the clinics, including those requested for patient care and for research. All patient records are computerized and tracked by a software system."

Maritza says, "What I like best about my work is knowing that we delivered the patient records to the institute clinics in a timely manner. I also like working with the NIH staff. There is never a dull moment."

This image shows a medical history under review. Each color corresponds to a different entity: doctor, insurance company, or legal entity.

few dangers exist. Laboratories are typically clean and well lit, but workers spend a great deal of time on their feet.

Hours and shifts depend on the size and type of facility. In large hospitals or other laboratories that operate continuously, technicians usually work a day, evening, or night shift and may work some weekends and holidays. Smaller facilities may offer rotating shifts, rather than regular shifts.

MEDICAL RECORDS AND HEALTH INFORMATION
TECHNICIANS

Medical records and health information technicians work with patients' health information, including medical history, symptoms, examination results, diagnostic tests, and treatment methods. They organize and manage all this data by verifying its quality and accuracy. These technicians also make sure this vital information is private, but that it is accessible when needed. They regularly work with doctors and other healthcare professionals to clarify diagnoses or to obtain additional information.

Because of an increase in the use of electronic health records (EHRs), job requirements for health information technicians increasingly include knowledge of computer software. Technicians use EHR software to maintain data on patient safety, patterns of disease, and disease treatment and outcome. Health information technicians also assist with improving EHR software and may contribute to the development and maintenance of health information networks.

MEDICAL CODERS

Some medical records and health information technicians specialize in codifying medical information for insurance reimbursement purposes. These technicians are called medical coders or coding specialists. Medical coders assign a code to each diagnosis and procedure by using classification systems software. The classification system determines the amount for which healthcare providers will be reimbursed if the patient is covered by Medicare, Medicaid, or other insurance programs using the system.

CANCER REGISTRY

Medical records and health information technicians may also specialize in cancer registry. Cancer (or tumor) registrars maintain databases of cancer patients. Registrars review patient records

Emergency medical technicians, more commonly known as EMTs, transport patients to the hospital in the case of an emergency. They are also responsible for transporting patients between medical facilities.

and pathology reports, and assign codes for the diagnosis and treatment of different cancers and selected benign tumors. Registrars contact patients annually to track treatment, survival, and recovery. This information is used to calculate survivor rates and success rates of various types of treatment, to locate geographic areas with high incidences of certain cancers, and to identify potential participants for clinical drug trials.

WORK ENVIRONMENT

Medical records and health information technicians work in offices. This is one of the few health-related occupations in which there is no direct hands-on patient care.

EMERGENCY MEDICAL TECHNICIANS AND PARAMEDICS

In emergency medical situations, people's lives may depend on the work of emergency medical technicians (EMTs) and paramedics. These technicians provide medical care during emergencies like car accidents, heart attacks, or childbirth.

A 911 operator sends EMTs and paramedics to the scene of an emergency, where they often work with police and fire fighters. Once they arrive, EMTs and paramedics assess the patient's condition, determine if the patient has any pre-existing medical conditions, provide emergency care, and transport the patient to a medical facility.

EMTs and paramedics generally work in teams. One team member drives, while the other monitors a patient's vital signs and gives additional care as needed. Upon arrival at the medical facility, EMTs and paramedics help transfer patients to the emergency department, report observations and actions, and sometimes provide additional emergency treatment. EMTs and paramedics may also transport patients from one medical facility to another.

Specific responsibilities depend on the level of qualification and training. The National Registry of Emergency Medical Technicians (NREMT) certifies emergency medical technicians at five levels: First Responder; EMT-Basic; EMT-Intermediate (which has two levels called 1985 and 1999), and Paramedic.

FIRST RESPONDER

These technicians are the first on a scene. Usually part of a fire department or other response team, first responders assess patients and stabilize them until more highly trained medical technicians can arrive.

EMT-BASIC

EMT-Basic represents the first response of the emergency medical system. An EMT trained at this level is prepared to care for patients at the scene of an accident and while transporting patients by ambulance to the hospital under the supervision of more highly trained medical personnel.

EMT-INTERMEDIATE

An EMT trained at the intermediate level has more advanced training. However, the specific tasks allowed vary from state to state.

Paramedics and EMTs take classes and run through hands-on simulated situations to prepare for real life emergencies.

What Kind of Person Are You?

Career-counseling experts know that certain kinds of people do best in certain kinds of jobs. John L. Holland developed the following list of personality types and the kinds of jobs that are the best match for each type. See which one (or two) are most like you. The more you understand yourself, the better you'll be able to make a good career plan for yourself.

- Realistic personality: This kind of person likes to do practical, hands-on work. He or she will most enjoy working with materials that can be touched and manipulated, such as wood, steel, tools, and machinery. This personality type enjoys jobs that require working outdoors, but he or she does NOT enjoy jobs that require a lot of paperwork or close teamwork with others.
- Investigative personality: This personality type likes to work with ideas. He or she will enjoy jobs that require lots of thinking and researching. Jobs that require mental problem solving will be a good fit for this personality.
- Artistic personality: This type of person enjoys working with forms, designs, and patterns. She or he likes jobs that require self-expression—and that don't require following a definite set of rules.
- Social personality: Jobs that require lots of teamwork with others, as well as teaching others, are a good match for this personality type. These jobs often involve helping others in some way.
- Enterprising personality: This person will enjoy planning and starting new projects, even if that involves a degree of risk-taking. He or she is good at making decisions and leading others.
- Conventional personality: An individual with this type of personality likes to follow a clear set of procedures or routines. He or she doesn't want to be the boss but prefers to work under someone else's leadership. Jobs that require working with details and facts (more than ideas) are a good fit for this personality.

PARAMEDIC

Paramedics are the most highly trained emergency medical technicians. They perform the procedures of the lower levels, but they can also administer medications, interpret electrocardiograms (EKGs), perform endotracheal intubations, and use other complex equipment. However, like the intermediate level, what paramedics are permitted to do varies by state.

WORK ENVIRONMENT

EMTs and paramedics have to do a lot of kneeling, bending, and heavy lifting. They risk hearing loss from sirens and back injuries from lifting patients. In addition, they may be exposed to dangerous diseases, and to violence from some patients. The work is physically strenuous and can be mentally stressful. Nonetheless, many people find the work exciting and challenging, and enjoy the opportunity to help others.

To ignore or discount your own values when making a career choice is to sell yourself short.

—Laurence G. Boldt

ABOUT THE QUOTE

What is the most important thing to you in life right now? What do you value most in others? What do you like best about yourself? What makes you happiest? Think about the answers to these questions as you consider which career path is right for you. And then think about these questions as well: What do you dislike doing most in life? What things in the world around you make you angriest? What would you avoid if you could? The career you choose should either allow you to avoid what you hate—or give you opportunities to change it.

CHAPTER 2
THE IMPORTANCE OF MEDICAL TECHNICIANS

Words to Know

Demographics: Statistical data about a population and the types of groups within the population.

Life expectancy: The number of years an individual is likely to live.

Fertility rates: The average number of births per woman in a population.

Baby boomers: The generation of people born in the years following World War II, when there was an increase in birthrate.

Longevity: Long life.

Policy: A course of action followed by a government

We live in a constantly changing world. Climate change is threatening our environment and health, new advances in technology make cars more environmentally friendly, computers and cell phones keep friends and family close through virtual connections, and science is always discovering new ways to battle illness or extend life. With this constant flux, are there any predictions we can make about what the future will be like?

We may not be able to paint an exact picture of what the future will bring, but there are some things we can predict. One thing that most experts consider a fact is that more people will be living on the planet in the future. The world population is currently at almost 7 million, and it is expected to grow to almost 10 billion by 2050. This growing population, combined with changing *demographics*, will lead to a greater need for healthcare workers like medical technicians.

Did You Know?
The total population of the United States is currently about 308,000,000.

WHY IS THE POPULATION AGING?

According to the World Health Organization, the fastest growing segment in almost all countries is the over-sixty age group. This is due to a combination of increased *life expectancy* and lower *fertility rates*. According to the United States Census Bureau, the world's sixty-five and older population is projected to triple by midcentury, from 516 million in 2009 to 1.53 billion in 2050. In contrast, the population under fifteen is expected to increase by only 6 percent during the same period, from 1.83 billion to 1.93 billion.

The entire world is seeing an increase in this discrepancy between the older and younger generations. For example, in the United States, the population sixty-five and older is expected to more than double by 2050, rising from 39 million today to 89 million, but the under 15 population in the United States is expected to fall below the older population by that date, only increasing from 62 million today to 85 million.

Since 1998, the number of older Americans has increased by 13 percent, which is only slightly faster than the 12.4 percent increase for the under-sixty-five population. The concern for the future is that the *baby boomers* in the forty-five- to sixty-four-year-old age group (who will reach sixty-five over the next two decades) increased by 31 percent since 1998. Also, the "oldest old," the age group of eighty and over, is increasing more rapidly than the older population as a whole. In other words, the population of the United States—and the entire world—is aging.

Why Is an Aging Population a Public Health Concern?

So why is an aging population considered a public health problem? You might think instead that it's a public health success (since people are staying alive longer than ever before). In some ways, this increased *longevity* does represent human triumphs over disease and disaster. However, the shift in population age from a young population to an older one has many implications for public healthcare and *policy*.

Part of the public health concern has to do with the fact that an aging population will experience different types of illnesses. Older people are more likely to be troubled by chronic diseases, such as heart disease, cancer, and diabetes. Therefore an increase in the older population will equal an increase in chronic disease. In fact, according to the National Institute on Aging, in the next ten to fifteen years, the loss of health and life around the world will be greater from chronic diseases than from infectious or parasitic diseases.

The family structure and economic status of the aging generation also pose a public health concern. Lower fertility rates combined with the increase in an older population and the simultaneous reduction in the younger population will leave an increased number of older people alone in their final years. Traditionally, children or grandchildren cared for older people in their declining years. However, in the future, many of the older generation will not have children or grandchildren to provide this care. In addition, increased rates of divorce and separation will leave many older men and women without a system of monetary or social support. Non-married older women are less likely to have accumulated wealth for use in old age, while non-married older men are less likely to have formed a strong social support system.

Did You Know?
Since 1900, the percentage of Americans over 65 years old has tripled, from 4.1% in 1900 to 12.8% in 2008.

All these issues will lead to a need for increased public support for the older generation. An increased number of health service centers will be needed to provide care to the older population. Chronic diseases require regular monitoring to prevent negative effects on the overall quality of life. Also, the increase in older people who are without family support may require an increase in the number of long-term nursing care facilities.

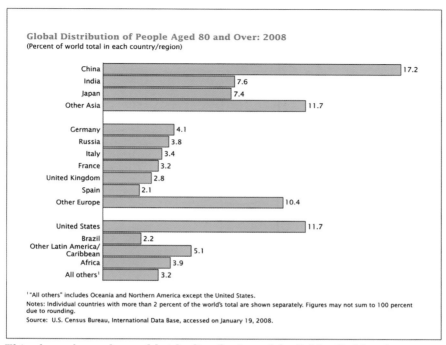

This chart shows the worldwide distribution of the "oldest" old—the population over 80 years old.

NEEDED: MORE HEALTHCARE WORKERS

The increase in an older population will result in an overall increase in the demand for healthcare workers. For example, according to the United States Department of Health and Human Services, if health-care consumption patterns and physician productivity remain constant over time, the aging population would increase the need

Did You Know?

There were 92,127 persons who were 100 or more in 2008!

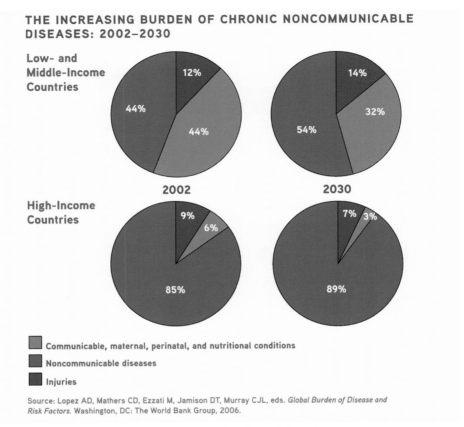

THE INCREASING BURDEN OF CHRONIC NONCOMMUNICABLE DISEASES: 2002–2030

Low- and Middle-Income Countries

2002 — 12%, 44%, 44%

2030 — 14%, 32%, 54%

High-Income Countries

2002 — 9%, 6%, 85%

2030 — 7%, 3%, 89%

- Communicable, maternal, perinatal, and nutritional conditions
- Noncommunicable diseases
- Injuries

Source: Lopez AD, Mathers CD, Ezzati M, Jamison DT, Murray CJL, eds. *Global Burden of Disease and Risk Factors*. Washington, DC: The World Bank Group, 2006.

Older people tend to carry a heavier burden of chronic diseases such as heart disease, cancer, and diabetes. Therefore, an increase in the older population will lead to an increase in chronic diseases around the world.

for physicians per thousand people from 2.8 in 2000 to 3.1 in 2020; demand for RNs per thousand people would increase from 7 to 7.5 during this same period. It is not only doctors and nurses who will be needed; projected employment growth is expected to be excellent for all divisions in the healthcare industry.

In general, medical technicians will see an increase in job opportunities over the next decade. Job opportunities for medical records technicians will be excellent, since as the incidence of cancer increases, there will be an increased need for cancer registrars. Emergency medical technicians will also see increased job opportunities as a large segment of the population becomes more likely to have medical emergencies. Also, with more elderly people receiving care from nursing facilities, there will be an increased need for EMTs and ambulances to transport patients between care centers. As a result of the projected growth in these fields, a young student considering a career as a medical technician can look forward to excellent job opportunities in the future.

Did You Know?
China has the largest older population—106 million in 2008. Japan is the "oldest" country, with 22% of its population 65 or older.

If You Have an Investigative Personality . . .

You may be happy in medical technician jobs where you have opportunities to understand and solve health problems. Be aware, though, that you will usually be working under higher-level medical professionals, who will be the ones ultimately responsible for carrying out any solutions you discover.

One way or another, we all have to find what best fosters the flowering of our humanity in this contemporary life, and dedicate ourselves to that.

—Joseph Campbell

ABOUT THE QUOTE

As you choose a career path, it's important to do your research. Read books like this one, talk to your guidance counselor, seek out information on the Internet. Have realistic expectations. But remember that while it's important to know the practical details involved with various careers, you also need to be sure that you will find satisfaction doing the work you choose. You should be able to know that you are contributing through your work to the human community, that in some small way you are making the world a better place.

CHAPTER 3
EDUCATION AND TRAINING

Words to Know

Associate degree: The degree given to a student who completes two years of study, usually given by community colleges.

Vocational school: A school that provides an education focused on a certain occupation and its skills.

Clinical: Involved with or based on direct interaction with patients.

Terminology: The vocabulary of technical terms used in a particular field or science.

Anatomy: The study of the human body and its parts.

Physiology: The scientific study of an organism's vital functions, including growth and development and the functioning of different tissues, organs, and other anatomic structures. Physiology studies the normal mechanical, physical, and biochemical processes of animals and plants.

Intravenous: Pertaining to a medicine that is given directly into a vein.

The level of education and training required to become a medical technician is dependent on the specific field that interests you. When choosing a field, you should first consider where your talents lie. If you enjoy science, especially laboratory-oriented experiments, then a career as a clinical laboratory technician might be fulfilling. However, if working directly with patients and helping to save lives is more appealing, then you might be better suited for a career in the emergency medical field. In either case, there are specific training and education requirements.

CLINICAL LABORATORY TECHNICIANS AND TECHNOLOGISTS

If laboratory work interests you, you can become a *clinical* laboratory technician by completing two years of training at a community college or a clinical laboratory scientist with a bachelor's degree or master's degree. Clinical laboratory technologists generally require a degree in medical technology or in one of the life sciences, such as biology. However, some jobs allow for a combination of education and on-the-job specialized training.

University degree programs in medical technology include courses in chemistry, biological sciences, microbiology, mathematics, and statistics, as well as specialized courses devoted to the knowledge and skills used in a clinical laboratory. Many programs also offer or require courses in management, business, and computer applications.

Laboratory technicians usually have either an *associate degree* from a community or junior college or certification from a hos-

Internships provide students with an opportunity to gain hands-on laboratory experience in a real laboratory setting.

pital, a *vocational school*, or the military. Some technicians are trained on the job.

LICENSURE

Some states require laboratory personnel to be licensed or registered to perform clinical laboratory work. This often requires a bachelor's degree and the passing of an exam, but requirements vary by state and specialty.

CERTIFICATION

Applicants certified by a recognized professional association are often preferred by possible employers. Associations offering certification include the Board of Registry of the American Society for Clinical Pathology, the American Medical Technologists, the

National Credentialing Agency for Laboratory Personnel, and the Board of Registry of the American Association of Bioanalysts.

OTHER JOB REQUIREMENTS

In addition to education and certification, employers look for lab workers with good judgment and the ability to work under pressure. Technologists in particular are expected to be good at problem solving. Close attention to detail is also important because small differences in test substances or variations in numerical readouts can alter a diagnosis. Finally, because of the widespread use of automated laboratory equipment, excellent computer skills are important for all laboratory technicians and technologists.

> **Did You Know?**
> Normal color vision is a highly desirable trait for clinical laboratory workers—many lab results depend on slight differences in the color of a liquid or test strip, so an ability to discern the correct colors is vital.

ADVANCEMENT

Technicians can advance and become technologists through additional education and experience. Professional certification and a graduate degree in medical technology, one of the biological sciences, chemistry, management, or education usually speeds advancement. Technologists may advance to supervisory positions, or may become chief medical or clinical laboratory technologists or laboratory managers in hospitals. A doctoral degree is usually required to become a laboratory director.

MEDICAL RECORDS AND HEALTH INFORMATION TECHNICIANS

Entry-level medical records and health information technicians usually have an associate degree from a community or junior college. Community colleges are good places to learn job skills for a number of reasons. They have low tuition and an open-admissions policy, and they offer many courses, including classes that will help prepare students for a career in health information technology. Typical coursework in health information technology includes medical *terminology*, *anatomy* and *physiology*, health data requirements and standards, clinical classification and coding systems, data analysis, healthcare reimbursement methods, database security and management, and quality improvement methods.

Community colleges are also flexible; at most community colleges, nearly 50 percent of the students work full time, so they offer courses at convenient times. Many workers choose a community college when they want to enter a new field or upgrade their skills in order to advance their career. A person with a college degree often attends a community college to update work skills.

CERTIFICATION

Most employers prefer to hire credentialed medical record and health information technicians. A number of organizations offer credentials typically based on passing a exam. Most credentialing programs require regular recertification and continuing education to maintain the credential. Many coding credentials require an amount of time in coding experience in the work setting.

Registered Apprenticeship

A Registered apprenticeship links formal instruction in the form of a degree or certification with on-the-job learning guided by a mentor. The apprentice goes through a structured, paid program until he or she completes the course of training. A registered apprenticeship offers a proven method that allows an employer to establish the standards required of its professionals.

The time requirements and content of an apprenticeship are dependent on the occupation. However, apprentices in every occupation are provided diverse and complex training that helps them become highly skilled in their chosen careers.

Some apprentice-able health care occupations are:

- ambulance attendant
- certified nursing assistant
- dental laboratory technician
- medical laboratory technician
- medical transcriptionists
- optician
- orthotics technician
- paramedic
- pharmacy technician
- prosthetics technician
- biomedical equipment technician
- dental assistant
- emergency medical technician (EMT)
- medical secretary
- nurse, licensed practical
- orthodontic technician
- orthotist
- pharmacist assistant
- podiatric assistant
- surgical technologist

Many health care occupations currently use an apprenticeship model for training without calling it that.

The American Health Information Management Association (AHIMA) offers credentialing as a registered health information technician (RHIT). To obtain the RHIT credential, an individual must graduate from a two-year associate degree program accredited by the Commission on Accreditation for Health Informatics and Information Management Education (CAHIIM) and pass an AHIMA-administered written examination.

The American Academy of Professional Coders (AAPC) offers coding credentials. The Board of Medical Specialty Coding (BMSC) and Professional Association of Health Care Coding Specialists (PAHCS) both offer credentialing in specialty coding. The National Cancer Registrars Association (NCRA) offers a credential as a certified tumor registrar (CTR).

Other Job Requirements

Excellent oral and written communication skills are vital for medical records and health information technicians, since they often carry communications between health-care facilities and insurance companies. As more health-care facilities adopt electronic health records, technicians with strong computer skills will be most appealing to employers. Finally, medical records and health information technicians should enjoy learning, as continuing education is important to keep up with and advance in the field.

Advancement

Experienced medical records and health information technicians usually advance their careers by obtaining a bachelor's or master's degree or by seeking an advanced specialty certification. Technicians with a bachelor's or master's degree can advance and become a health information manager.

Emergency Medical Technicians and Paramedics

A high school diploma is required to enter a training program to become an EMT or paramedic. Workers must complete a formal training and certification process. The training is progressive, meaning each level of training becomes more advanced.

EMT-Basic

Basic level training emphasizes basic emergency skills, such as managing respiratory, trauma and cardiac emergencies, and patient assessment. Classroom studies are often combined with clinical hours in an emergency department or ambulance. The program provides instruction and practice in dealing with bleeding, fractures, airway obstruction, cardiac arrest, and emergency childbirth. Students learn how to use and maintain common emergency equipment, such as backboards, suction devices, splints, oxygen delivery systems, and stretchers. Graduates of approved EMT-Basic training programs must pass a written and practical examination administered by a state licensing agency or the NREMT.

EMT-Intermediate

Intermediate level training requirements vary by state. The nationally defined levels, EMT-Intermediate 1985 and EMT-

Intermediate 1999, typically require 30 to 350 hours of training based on scope of practice. Students learn advanced skills such as the use of advanced airway devices, *intravenous* fluids, and some medications.

PARAMEDIC

At this most advanced level, the EMT receives training in anatomy and physiology, as well as advanced medical skills. Most commonly, the training is conducted in community colleges and technical schools, and may result in an associate's degree. These programs may take one to two years. The coursework prepares the student to take the NREMT examination to become certified

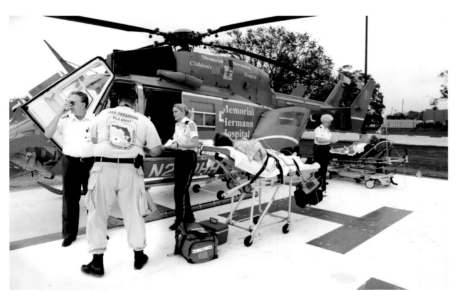

An air ambulance is an aircraft, often a helicopter, used in emergency situations when a standard ambulance can't reach the area, or the patient needs faster transport than a standard ambulance can provide.

as a paramedic. Extensive coursework, as well as clinical and field experience, is required. Refresher courses and continuing education are available (and usually required) for EMTs and paramedics at all levels.

LICENSURE

All fifty U.S. states require EMTs and paramedics to be licensed, but

Did You Know?
Many states restrict EMT licensure if an individual has a criminal history.

the levels and titles vary from state to state. In most states and the District of Columbia, certification by the NREMT is required

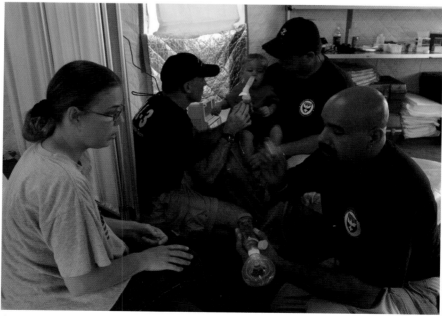

Some EMTs continue to provide care to their patients even after the patients have been brought to an emergency room.

at some or all levels. Some states administer their own certification examination or provide the option of taking either the NREMT or state examination. In most states, licensure renewal is required every two to three years, and EMTs and paramedics must generally take refresher training courses or complete continuing education requirements.

OTHER JOB REQUIREMENTS

EMTs and paramedics need to be physically fit, mentally and emotionally stable, have good physical coordination, and be able to lift and carry heavy loads.

ADVANCEMENT

Paramedics can become supervisors, operations managers, administrative directors, or executive directors of emergency services. Some EMTs and paramedics become instructors, dispatchers, or physician assistants; others move into sales or marketing of emergency medical equipment. A number of people become EMTs and paramedics to test their interest in health care before training as registered nurses, physicians, or other health workers.

If You Have a Social Personality . . .

You may enjoy medical technician positions that allow you to work directly with patients. These jobs will give you opportunities to help people who need you. Your helpful, friendly nature will be an asset for you as you work with patients.

All labor . . .
has dignity and
importance
and should be
undertaken with
painstaking
excellence.

—Martin Luther
King Jr.

ABOUT THE QUOTE

No matter what job you choose, do it well. Even if you end up settling for a lower-paid position than what you'd hope to find, do your job well. Even the smallest jobs are important to the big picture and contribute to the world where we live. Besides, you never know what experiences will be useful to you in the future. Even the most boring jobs can lead you to new opportunities that are just right for you. And remember, if you always do your best, people will notice—which means those new opportunities are more likely to come along.

CHAPTER 4

JOB OPPORTUNITIES AND RELATED OCCUPATIONS

S o you've decided to become a medical technician, and you've started down the appropriate education path. What happens after graduation or the completion of training? What jobs are available and how do you find them?

CLINICAL LABORATORY TECHNOLOGISTS AND TECHNICIANS

Clinical laboratory technologists and technicians held about 328,100 jobs in 2008. More than half of these jobs were in hospitals. Most of the remaining jobs were in doctors' offices and in medical laboratories. A small proportion of the jobs were in educational services. Businesses that make home testing kits, laboratory equipment, or medical supplies also hired experienced technologists to work in product development, marketing, and sales.

MEDICAL RECORDS AND HEALTH INFORMATION TECHNICIANS

Medical records and health information technicians held about 172,500 jobs in 2008. About 39 percent of these jobs were in hospitals. Health information technicians also work at health-care providers, such as doctor's offices, nursing care facilities, outpatient care centers, and home health-care services. The federal government also employs some medical records technicians.

EMERGENCY MEDICAL TECHNICIANS AND PARAMEDICS

EMTs and paramedics held about 210,700 jobs in 2008. Most career EMTs and paramedics work in large cities. Volunteer EMTs and paramedics are more common in small cities, towns, and rural areas. These individuals volunteer for fire departments, emergency medical services, or hospitals and may respond to only a few calls per month.

RELATED OCCUPATIONS

Perhaps you are interested in science and medicine, but none of these technician positions sound just right. Unless you know for sure you are interested in a more familiar health-care career, you might want to consider another related job.

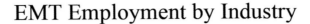

EMT Employment by Industry

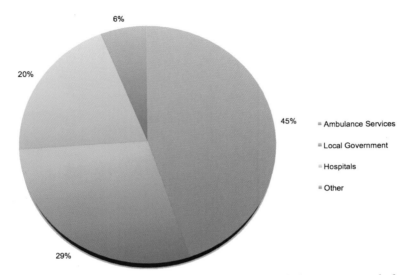

6%

20%

45%   ▪ Ambulance Services

▪ Local Government

▪ Hospitals

▪ Other

29%

The majority of emergency medical technicians work for private ambulance services, as opposed to ambulance companies owned and operated by hospitals or towns.

CLINICAL LABORATORY TECHNICIANS AND TECHNOLOGISTS

CHEMISTS AND MATERIALS SCIENTISTS

Everything in the environment, whether naturally occurring or of human design, is composed of chemicals. Chemists and materials scientists search for new knowledge about chemicals and use it to improve life. Chemical research has led to the discovery and development of thousands of commonly used products. Chemists and materials scientists also develop processes such as improved oil refining and petrochemical processing that save energy and reduce pollution. An environmental application of materials

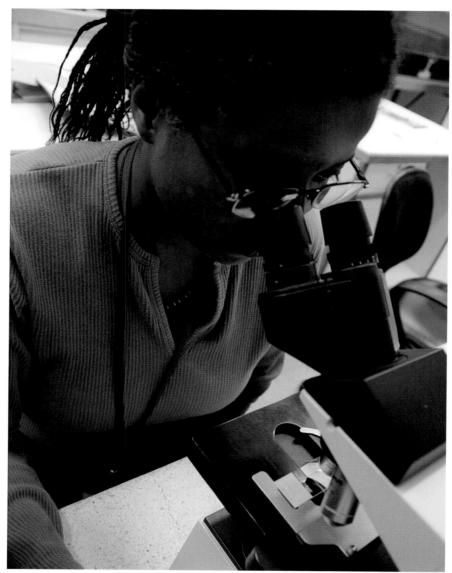

Good laboratory skills and the proper training will make you eligible for technician positions in a wide range of science laboratories.

science is the development of better, more efficient fuel cells. Research on the chemistry of living things spurs advances in medicine, agriculture, and food processing, as well as environmental science.

SCIENCE TECHNICIANS

Science technicians are the laborers of the science industry. They assist scientists in research and development, and help to invent and improve products and processes. Their jobs are more practically oriented than those of scientists. In other words, scientists develop ideas, and the technicians do the work that tests or develops those ideas into real-world applications. Most science technicians specialize in a particular field, learning their skills and working in the same disciplines in which scientists work.

VETERINARY TECHNOLOGISTS AND TECHNICIANS

If you dream of working with animals but are not ready to commit to the lengthy education required to become a veterinarian, then a career as a veterinary technologist or technician might be a perfect fit. Veterinary technicians are to veterinarians what nurses are to doctors. They work under the supervision of a licensed veterinarian, perform various medical tests, and treat and diagnose medical conditions and diseases in animals. Vet techs may perform laboratory tests such as urinalysis and blood counts, assist with dental care, prepare tissue samples, take blood samples, and assist veterinarians in a variety of other diagnostic tests. Besides these lab-based jobs, some veterinary technicians record patients' case histories, expose and develop X-rays and

Real-Life Medical Technician

Darryl Lowery is an EMT with the National Institutes of Health Fire Department in Bethesda, Maryland. A positive volunteer experience with his local fire department sent him on the path to this career at the age of only sixteen.

As a volunteer, he took first-aid classes and became certified in CPR. After graduating from high school, he took emergency medical services courses at the University of Maryland. The courses included 144 classroom hours and 20 hours of clinical training through the Maryland Fire and Rescue Institute (MFRI). At the end of all this studying, Darryl took and passed the state certification test. However, his training is never complete because he must take a refresher course every three years and pass another exam to maintain his certification.

Darryl loves his job, but he knows that his career as a firefighter and EMT is limited since federal firefighters have to retire at age fifty-seven. The physical demands of the job are harder to bear as EMTs grow older. Darryl is already planning for the next phase of his career: he is working toward a bachelor's degree in fire science, which is the study of fire's behavior, the effectiveness of fire retardants, and other aspects of fire.

radiographs, and provide specialized nursing care. In addition, experienced veterinary technicians may discuss a pet's condition with its owners or train new clinic personnel.

MEDICAL RECORDS TECHNICIANS

MEDICAL AND HEALTH SERVICES MANAGERS

Medical and health services managers help keep the business side of health care running smoothly. Also referred to as health-care executives or health-care administrators, these workers plan, direct, coordinate, and supervise the delivery of health care. They may be in charge of a specific department or manage an entire facility or system.

MEDICAL TRANSCRIPTIONISTS

Medical transcriptionists listen to dictated recordings made by doctors and other healthcare workers and *transcribe* them into medical reports, correspondence, and other written documents, which eventually become part of patients' permanent files. The documents they transcribe include discharge summaries, medical history and physical examination reports, operation reports, consultation reports, *autopsy* reports, diagnostic-imaging studies, progress notes, and referral letters.

If You Have a Realistic Personality . . .

Being a medical technician may be a good choice for you, since you can probably find a job setting where you will work with tools and machines, allowing you to express the practical and mechanical side of your nature.

Fear always springs from ignorance.

—Ralph Waldo Emerson

ABOUT THE QUOTE

The point in your life where you stand at the ultimate edge of childhood ready to step forward into adulthood can be a scary place. You face new responsibilities and new challenges; you will encounter countless new people who will have new expectations of you; and although adulthood will bring new freedoms, it will also bring new restrictions—long work days, bills to pay, and other obligations. But what makes it all look so frightening is usually simply the fact that it's unknown. So do your homework! Research your career interests in books like this and on the Internet. Talk to as many people as you can who are already in the work world. The more you know what to expect, the more prepared you will be for what lies ahead—and the less scary it will seem.

CHAPTER 5
THE FUTURE FOR MEDICAL TECHNICIANS

Words to Know
Ambulatory: Capable of walking; ambulatory healthcare centers care for patients who are able to walk in for treatment.
Mentor: Train and offer advice to a student.
Prospective: Referring to something that is potential or possible in the future.

JOB OUTLOOK

In general, the job outlook for careers in the healthcare industry is excellent. In fact, the healthcare industry is predicted to add nearly 4 million new jobs between 2006 and 2016, and have the fastest annual growth rate of all career industries.

As the country's population ages, there is a rising need to fill many essential health-care positions. No matter the region of the country or the community, the need for skilled workers is likely to be high in all specialties within the health-care industry.

CLINICAL LABORATORY TECHNICIANS AND TECHNOLOGISTS

Rapid job growth and excellent job opportunities are expected for technicians and technologists in clinical laboratories, because the number of job openings is predicted to continue to exceed the number of jobseekers. Hospitals are expected to continue to hire the highest percentage of clinical laboratory workers, but employment is also expected to grow rapidly in medical and diagnostic laboratories, doctor's offices, and all other *ambulatory* healthcare services.

Employment for clinical laboratory workers is expected to grow by 14 percent between 2008 and 2018, faster than the average of

The demand for skilled laboratory workers is expected to increase job opportunities for medical laboratory technicians and technologists over the next decade.

11 percent for all occupations. In large part, this will be due to an increase in the number of laboratory tests needed as population growth increase. In addition, the development of new types of tests will change the workload for laboratory technicians. In contradiction to the overall growth of the field, the automation and simplification of some tests may actually decrease the need for laboratory technicians.

MEDICAL RECORDS AND HEALTH INFORMATION TECHNICIANS

Job prospects for medical records and health information technicians should be very good. Technicians with a strong understanding of technology and computer software will be especially attractive to employers.

Employment for medical records and health information technicians is expected to grow by 20 percent, much faster than the average for all occupations through 2018. This growth will result from the increase in the number of medical tests, treatments, and procedures that will be performed. In addition, as the population continues to age, the occurrence of health-related problems, such as cancer, will increase. Finally, the increasing use of electronic health records will require more technicians to handle the increased data management responsibilities.

Occupational Title	SOC Code	Employment, 2008	Projected Employment, 2018	Change, 2008–18	
				Number	Percent
Clinical laboratory technologists and technicians	29-2010	328,100	373,600	45,600	14
Medical and clinical laboratory technologists	29-2011	172,400	193,000	20,500	12
Medical and clinical laboratory technicians	29-2012	155,600	180,700	25,000	16

Occupational Title	SOC Code	Employment, 2008	Projected Employment, 2018	Change, 2008-18	
				Number	Percent
Medical records and health information technicians	29-2071	172,500	207,600	35,100	20

Occupational Title	SOC Code	Employment, 2008	Projected Employment, 2018	Change, 2008-18	
				Number	Percent
Emergency medical technicians and paramedics	29-2041	210,700	229,700	19,000	9

As can be seen from these tables as well as the table on page 57, the employment growth rate over the next decade is expected to be highest for medical records technicians.

EMERGENCY MEDICAL TECHNICIANS AND PARAMEDICS

Job prospects for EMTs and paramedics should be good, especially in cities and private ambulance services. More paid EMTs and paramedics will be needed to replace unpaid volunteers. Fewer people are volunteering as EMTs because of the amount of training and the large time commitment these positions require. EMTs and paramedics with advanced education or certifications will be the most attractive to employers.

Overall, employment for EMTs and paramedics is expected to grow about 9 percent between 2008 and 2018, which is about as fast as the average for all occupations. This growth is due in large part to increasing call volume due to the aging population. In addition, the time that EMTs and paramedics spend with each patient is expected to increase as emergency departments across the country experience overcrowding. As more time is spent with each patient, more EMTs and ambulances will be needed to meet call demands. In addition, more ambulances and EMTs will be needed to meet increasing needs to transport patients between specialized hospitals and treatment centers.

PLANNING FOR THE FUTURE

The information in this book is meant to be only an introduction to the health-care industry and to some of the career opportunities available for medical technicians and related fields. If you think you are interested in becoming a medical technician, it is never too early to start learning your options or to begin gaining experience.

- Speak to a school guidance counselor to get advice on how to find student job opportunities in your area.

- A science teacher or even a local medical technician may be able to *mentor* you or offer additional instruction in proper equipment use or laboratory procedure.

- Find out if your high school or town offers training in first aid or emergency services. After some training, you may even be able to volunteer with your local fire department or ambulance squad.

Everything you do that is related to your interest in a health-care career will help guide you to the specialization for which you are most suited and will strengthen you in the eyes of *prospective* schools or employers.

If You Have an Enterprising Personality . . .

Being a medical technician may not be the best career choice for you, since you would have few opportunities to lead others. Your level of ambition might be frustrated working in jobs where you are expected to provide support to others who have higher-paid and more prestigious positions.

If You Have a Conventional Personality . . .

Being a medical technician could be an excellent career choice for you. You'll have plenty of opportunities to work with numbers, records, and machines in a set, orderly way. Since you're good at working with written records and numbers in a systematic, orderly way, you'll do well as a medical technician.

FURTHER READING

Department of Economic and Social Affairs—Population Division. World Population Ageing: 1950–2050. United Nations, 2002.

FIND OUT MORE ON THE INTERNET

American Medical Technologists
www.amt1.com

American Society for Clinical Pathology
www.ascp.org/FunctionalNavigation/certification.aspx

Career Compass
www.careervoyages.gov/careercompass-main.cfm

Explore Health Careers
www.explorehealthcareers.org/en/Career.43.aspx

Job Corps
www.jobcorps.gov/home.aspx

Medical Training Directory
www.medicaltrainingdirectory.com

National Registry of Emergency Medical Technicians
www.nremt.org

States' Career Clusters
www.careerclusters.org

U.S. College Search
www.uscollegesearch.org

DISCLAIMER

BIBLIOGRAPHY

Career Voyages. "Health Care-Apprenticeship," www.careervoyages. gov/healthcare-apprenticeshipws.cfm (22 March 2010).

National Institute on Aging. "Why Population Aging Matters: A Global Perspective." National Institutes of Health, Publication No. 07-6134, March 2007.

National Institutes of Health, LifeWorks. "Meet a Real Technician, Emergency Medical, and Paramedic: Darrly Lowery," www.science.education.nih.gov/LifeWorks.nsf/Interviews/Darryl+Lowery (22 March 2010).

National Institutes of Health, LifeWorks. "Meet a Real Technician, Medical Records and Health Information: Maritza Sinclair," www. science.education.nih.gov/LifeWorks.nsf/Interviews/Maritza+Sinclair (22 March 2010).

United States Bureau of Labor Statistics. "Clinical Laboratory Technologists and Technicians," www.bls.gov/oco/ocos096.htm (16 March 2010).

United States Bureau of Labor Statistics. "Emergency Medical Technicians and Paramedics," www.bls.gov/oco/ocos101.htm (16 March 2010).

United States Bureau of Labor Statistics. "Medical Records and Health Information Technicians," www.bls.gov/oco/ocos103.htm (16 March 2010).

United States Census Bureau. "Census Bureau Reports World's Older Population Projected to Triple by 2050," www.census.gov/Press-Release/www/releases/archives/international_population/013882.html (23 March 2010).

United States Department of Health and Human Services. "A Profile of Older Americans: 2009," www.aoa.gov/AoARoot/Aging_Statistics/Profile/2009/3.aspx (23 March 2010).

United States Department of Health and Human Services. "Changing Demographics and the Implications for Physicians, Nurses and Other Health Workers," www.bhpr.hrsa.gov/healthworkforce/reports/changedemo/aging.htm (23 March 2010).

World Health Organization. "Ageing," www.who.int/topics/ageing/en/ (23 March 2010).

World Health Organization. "Our Ageing World," www.who.int/ageing/en/index.html (23 March 2010).

INDEX

PICTURE CREDITS

About the Author

Cordelia Strange has a master's degree from Binghamton University and is especially interested in health, the environment, and education. She enjoys applying these interests (and others) in writing books for young people.

About the Consultant

Michael Puglisi is the director of the Department of Labor's Workforce New York One Stop Center in Binghamton, New York. He has also held several leadership positions in the International Association of Workforce Professionals (IAWP), a non-profit educational association exclusively dedicated to workforce professionals with a rich tradition and history of contributions to workforce excellence. IAWP members receive the tools and resources they need to effectively contribute to the workforce development system daily. By providing relevant education, timely and informative communication and valuable findings of pertinent research, IAWP equips its members with knowledge, information and practical tools for success. Through its network of local and regional chapters, IAWP is preparing its members for the challenges of tomorrow.